FANTASTIC FACTS ABOUT

MAMMALS

Author
Martin Walters

Editor
Steve Parker

Design
Pentacor

Image Coordination
Ian Paulyn

Production Assistant
Rachel Jones

Index
Janet de Saulles

Editorial Director
Paula Borton

Design Director
Clare Sleven

Publishing Director
Jim Miles

This is a Parragon Publishing Book

This edition is published in 2001

Parragon Publishing, Queen Street House, 4 Queen Street, Bath BA1 1HE, UK

Copyright Parragon © 2000

Parragon has previously printed this material in 1999 as part of the Factfinder series

2 4 6 8 10 9 7 5 3 1

Produced by Miles Kelly Publishing Ltd
Bardfield Centre, Great Bardfield, Essex CM7 4SL

ISBN 0-75254-876-X

Printed in China

FANTASTIC FACTS ABOUT

MAMMALS

p

CONTENTS

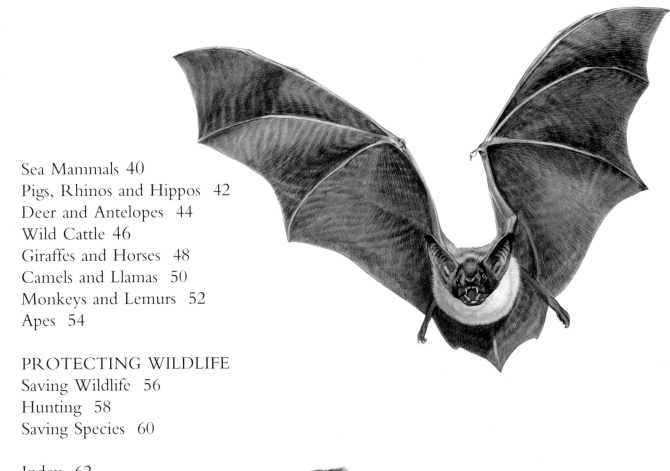

INTRODUCTION

A newborn kangaroo is only the size of a grape. Bats are mammals which fly; they navigate by sound, not sight. It can take a full month for a sloth to digest its food. Discover more about mammals—where they live, what they eat, and how they survive. Also find out what we can do to help protect threatened species, like the tiger, which face extinction.

MAMMALS is a handy reference guide in the *Fascinating Facts* series. Each book has been specially compiled with a collection of stunning illustrations and photographs which bring the subject to life. Hundreds of facts and figures are presented in a variety of interesting ways and side-panels which provide information at-a-glance. This unique combination is fun and easy to use and makes learning a pleasure.

MAMMALS

When asked to think of 'animals', most people think first of mammals. Yet mammals make up only a small number of species in the animal kingdom – about 4,150, compared with 9,000 bird species, 25,000 fish and more than one million insects.

The key feature of mammals is that the females feed their young on milk produced by the mother. Also, mammals are warm-blooded. (The only other warm-blooded animal group is the birds.) And mammal bodies have fur or hair, to keep in their body warmth.

Mammals which live in the water often have thick layers of fat under their skin, as extra insulation. The mammals also include a group

which have truly mastered flight, the bats.
(The only other two flying groups are birds
and insects.)

BIRTH AND BABIES
Some mammals, the marsupials, give birth
to babies which are at a very early stage of
development. But most mammals (about
nine-tenths of species) give birth to their
young at a more advanced stage. These are
known as placental mammals, after the body
part the placenta, which nourishes the
growing babies inside the mother's womb.

Some young mammals, such as guinea pigs
and antelopes, can run and feed soon
after being born. With others,
such as rabbits and cats, the
young are blind and
helpless at first.

LARGE MARSUPIALS

Marsupial mammals are named for the female's marsupium. This is the pocket or pouch on the female's chest or belly, where her young feed on her milk after they have been born. This is why marsupials are sometimes known as pouched mammals.

The best-known marsupials are kangaroos and their smaller relatives the wallabies. These have come to be symbols of their native land, Australia. They have muscular hind legs and bound along at enormous speed, using their thick tail to balance. The newborn baby kangaroo is only the size of a grape. It crawls through its mother's fur to her pouch, feeds on her milk, and develops rapidly. The older youngster leaves the pouch to explore, but scuttles back if danger threatens.

Large tail serves as third leg for resting

Young kangaroo is called a "joey"

GRAY KANGAROO
In some areas these kangaroos are pests, eating crops and natural vegetation.

COMMON IN THE GARDEN

Another familiar marsupial is the opossum of eastern North America. It feigns death—"plays possum"—when it is threatened by attack. It uses its long tail to hang from trees.

BOUNDING AND BOUNCING

The kangaroo's method of bounding along uses very little energy. The animal's joints and tendons work like elastic to store the energy from each jump, then they release the energy again to propel the kangaroo on its next bound.

Kangaroos have the longest feet in the animal kingdom

Mammals

4,150 species
- young fed on mother's milk
- body with fur or hair
- warm-blooded
- most have four limbs
- breathe through lungs

Main groups of mammals include:

Monotremes

3 species
- the only mammals that lay eggs
- adults are toothless
- Australia and New Guinea
- include platypus and echidnas (spiny anteaters)

Marsupials

270 species
- tiny, undeveloped young raised in mother's pouch
- live mainly in Australia, New Guinea, and South and Central America

SMALL MARSUPIALS

The cuddly-looking koala is one of the most appealing of all the marsupials. In fact, it has very sharp claws to help it cling onto tree branches and is less cuddly in real life. Koalas spend much of their time snoozing and most of the remaining time munching on eucalyptus leaves. They rarely come down to the ground.

A confirmed ground-dweller is the closely-related wombat, which digs a system of underground burrows. Both koalas and wombats look like small bears, but they are not related to true bears, they are marsupials. In fact, marsupials have evolved their own 'versions' of many other mammals. There are marsupial moles, marsupial mice and even marsupial rats.

HONEY POSSUM
This tiny marsupial lives on nectar and pollen from flowers, collected with its long snout and brush-tipped tongue.

KOALA AND YOUNG
Koalas are slow-moving and inoffensive – unless threatened, when they slash out with their sharp claws. They eat almost nothing but eucalyptus (gum) leaves. They hardly ever drink, obtaining moisture from the leaves.

GLIDERS

Several marsupials, known as gliders, can swoop in the air from tree to tree. They do this by using a parachute-like flap of skin stretching from the front to hind leg on either side of the body. The glider spreads out these flaps as it jumps.

MARSUPIAL MOLE
The female's pouch opens backwards, so it does not fill with soil as she tunnels.

Some of the main marsupial groups:

American opossums
75 species

Marsupial mice and relatives
53 species

Kangaroos and wallabies
50 species

Possums
23 species

Bandicoots
17 species

Brushtail possums and cuscuses
14 species

Ringtail possums, pygmy possums and gliders
30 species

Rat kangaroos
10 species

Wombats
3 species

Koala
1 species

13

SMALL RODENTS

The largest group by far of the placental mammals is the rodents, with some 1,600 species. They include hundreds of different species of mice, rats, voles, lemmings, jerboas, squirrels, chipmunks, beavers, and many others. A rodent's key feature is its sharp front teeth (incisors) that gnaw and chew through even the hardest foods, such as nuts or tree bark.

Some small rodents, for example mice, rats, hamsters, gerbils, and guinea pigs, have been domesticated and are often kept as pets.

MIGRATING LEMMINGS
Lemmings live in the cold northern lands of the tundra. Sometimes their populations build up to such a level that the lemmings eat all the food. So they must move on or migrate, often in huge numbers.

DORMOUSE
Some rodents hibernate, sleeping deeply through the cold season. The dormouse makes a grassy nest among tree roots. Its body becomes so cold that its ears and feet turn purple.

SMALL TO BIG

There are about 775 different kinds of mice and rats, ranging from the tiny pygmy mouse, which has a total length of 4 inches (10 cm), to large rats eight times as long. The harvest mouse is very agile and uses its long tail as an extra limb when clambering among grass stems.

NORWAY LEMMING
Lemmings stay active through the winter, digging tunnels under the snow to reach berries and seeds.

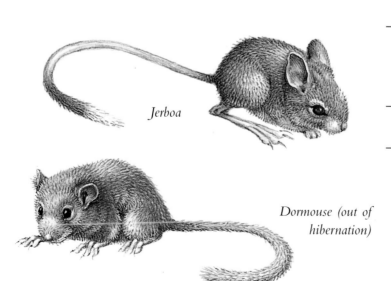

Jerboa

Dormouse (out of hibernation)

Rodents
1,600 species
- small to medium-sized placental mammals
- strong, chisel-shaped incisor teeth at front of mouth, for gnawing
- many are active at night
- very widespread and numerous (the house mouse is the most widespread mammal after the human being)

Main groups of smaller rodents include:

Pocket mice
65 species

Rats, mice, voles, hamsters, gerbils, and relatives
1,082 species

Dormice
10 species

Jerboas, jumping mice, and birch mice
45 species

LARGE RODENTS

Most rodents are small or medium-sized, but several groups contain larger species. Squirrels are adept climbers and spend most of their lives up in the trees, clinging on with sharp claws and using their furry tails to balance. 'Flying' squirrels cannot really fly, but glide well from tree to tree, using the stretched skin between front and back limbs.

Marmots and prairie dogs are like chunky, tail-less squirrels. They live in underground burrows. Beavers can measure 150 centimetres in total length. They swim well, using their webbed hind feet and flat rudder-like tail.

BEAVER
Beavers gnaw at trees to feed on the soft bark and young sap-rich wood just beneath. They cut down trees to eat the higher branches and also to use the logs for dam-building.

PORCUPINES

The porcupines have sharp spines, which are very thick hairs used for defence against predators. American porcupines live in trees and have long, prehensile tails to help them cling onto branches. European, African and Asian porcupines are ground-dwellers.

LODGE
The beaver's home is called a lodge. It is built in a lake created by the beavers damming a stream.

RED SQUIRREL
This type of squirrel has become rare in parts of Europe, partly because its natural conifer woodland home has been replaced by conifer plantations.

Groups of larger rodents include:

Squirrels, marmots and relatives
267 species

Porcupines
21 species

Cavies (guinea pigs)
14 species

Agoutis
13 species

Chinchillas
6 species

Beavers
2 species

Capybara
1 species

Coypu
1 species

Springhare
1 species

Largest rodent
• The capybara of South America measures up to 135 centimetres long and 60 centimetres tall at the shoulder.

ELEPHANTS

There are only two species of elephant: the African and the Asian. The African elephant has a larger body, bigger ears, longer tusks, and a less bumpy forehead.

African elephants live south of the Sahara Desert in savanna, forest, or dry scrubland. They roam in small family groups feeding on grass, bark, and twigs. They move slowly and steadily most of the time, walking at about the same speed as us. But a charging elephant can outrun a person, reaching a speed of 28 miles per hour (40 km/h) for a short sprint. The rumbling growl of an elephant can carry for more than a mile through the bush, and elephants use their deep voices to keep in touch. The tusks of an elephant are oversized incisor teeth and get larger through life.

Trained Asian elephant

Trunk is elongated nose and upper lip

Tusks trimmed for safety

AFRICAN ELEPHANT
Large male elephants usually live alone except during the mating season. If they feel in danger, they face the enemy and extend their ears to look even bigger than usual!

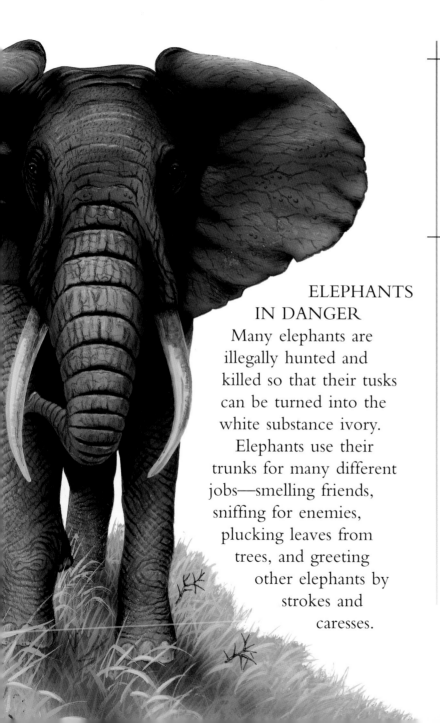

ELEPHANTS IN DANGER

Many elephants are illegally hunted and killed so that their tusks can be turned into the white substance ivory.

Elephants use their trunks for many different jobs—smelling friends, sniffing for enemies, plucking leaves from trees, and greeting other elephants by strokes and caresses.

Elephants

2 species

- African elephant is found scattered in Africa, mainly Central, East, and South
- Indian elephant is found in India, Sri Lanka, South China, Southeast Asia

Elephant records

- Elephants are the largest land animals. A big male African elephant can grow to almost 13 feet (4 m) tall at the shoulder and weigh more than 5 tons. His tusks can be over 10 feet (3 m) long.
- Elephants cool themselves down in hot weather by gently flapping their ears. The heat is lost to the air over a huge surface area from the blood vessels in the ears, which work like heating radiators in reverse.

BIGGER CATS

Lions are probably the best known of all the big cats, but there are six other members of the true big cat group: the tiger, jaguar, leopard, snow leopard, clouded leopard and cheetah. Most of the big cats are either spotted or striped, but the adult

Leopard

Black panther (a black variety of leopard)

Mountain lion

Jaguar

Lynx

Cheetah

Lions

lion is a uniform sandy colour, although lion cubs are spotted. The black panther is actually a very dark colour variety of the leopard. Black jaguars also occur. Big cats are active hunters of live prey, usually other mammals or birds.

LIVING TOGETHER

Lions are the only cats that live together, in family groups known as prides. They can tackle animals larger than themselves by working together to ambush their prey. They join in and gorge themselves on the meat, before sleeping it off until the next hunting foray.

The jaguar is unusual among cats, in that it eats a very varied diet that includes deer, monkeys, sloths, rodents, birds, turtles, frogs and plenty of fish.

The thick fur of the snow leopard gives it excellent insulation in the icy mountains of Asia, at heights of more than 5,000 metres.

BIG AND BIGGER

Four of the seven species of true big cats are shown here. So are some other cat species — including the mountain lion (also known as the puma or cougar) and the lynx.

Big cats

7 species

- Lion, lives in Africa, mainly in grasslands; very small population in India
- Tiger, lives in India, China, Indonesia, in forest, swamp and scrub
- Jaguar, lives in South and Central America, mainly in damp forests and swamps
- Leopard, lives in Africa and Southern Asia, in a wide variety of habitats from mountains to forests, swamps and semi-desert
- Snow leopard, lives in Asia, in uplands and mountains
- Clouded leopard, lives in Southeast Asia, in forests
- Cheetah, lives in Africa and south west Asia, mainly in grassland and dry scrub

Biggest big cat

- The Siberian type of tiger measures more than 3 metres from head to tail, and weighs over 300 kilograms.

21

SMALLER CATS

Whatever their size, big or small, most cats show similar behavior, especially when hunting. They work at night and alone. The cat stalks its prey quietly, keeping low near the ground. It then makes a quick dash to grab the victim, holding it down with sharp claws, biting and slashing. The cat often clamps its jaws and teeth onto the prey's neck, to close its windpipe until it suffocates.

CAT CLAWS

Cats are unusual among mammals in being able to pull their claws into fleshy toe sheaths when the claws are not needed. This keeps the claw points clean and sharp —and makes pet cats more comfortable to handle than dogs!

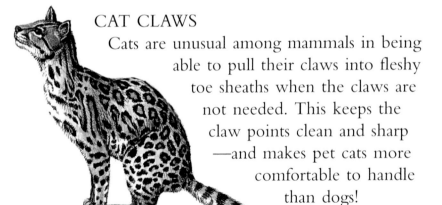

DOMESTIC CATS
The Abyssinian breed of domestic or pet cat is probably very similar to the original wild cats, from which all pet cats have been bred. The first domestic cats may have scavenged around human settlements more than 9,000 years ago.

MARGAY
One of about 20 species of smaller cat, the margay lives in Central and South American forests and scrub, hunting small animals such as rabbits, squirrels, rats, and birds.

BIGGER SMALL CATS

The lynx is one of the biggest small cats. It has well padded, heavily furred feet and long legs—adaptations that help it move through deep snow. The largest of the "small" cats is the puma. It may be more than 6 feet (1.8 m)

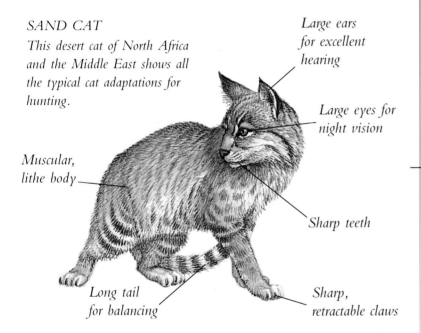

SAND CAT
This desert cat of North Africa and the Middle East shows all the typical cat adaptations for hunting.

Large ears for excellent hearing

Large eyes for night vision

Muscular, lithe body

Sharp teeth

Long tail for balancing

Sharp, retractable claws

long including its tail. Large pumas can even kill fully grown deer. Most species of smaller cats live in forests and have spotted coats for camouflage—which has led to themselves being hunted by people for their furs.

23

WOLVES AND FOXES

The dog family includes wolves, foxes and jackals. The familiar domesticated dogs, which have been bred into a huge number of different shapes and sizes, probably originated from the grey or timber wolf. Unlike cats, dogs tend to hunt in groups, called packs. Their long, powerful legs enable them to run well and for long periods.

The grey wolf is the largest of the dogs, found in forest, tundra and mountains. Wolves eat a wide range of food, from deer to small mammals, and even berries and other fruits. Even though they are common in some places, wolves are very rarely a danger to people.

RED OR COMMON FOX
This is one of the most adaptable and widespread of all mammals, living in remote country and also scavenging in towns and cities.

Australian wild dog or dingo

CALL OF THE WILD

Coyotes are common in parts of North America. They are rather like smaller versions of wolves and their eerie night howls are the 'call of the wild'. The maned wolf lives in tall grasslands in South America. It has long, graceful legs and attractive red-brown fur.

DOGGY MOODS
Like pet dogs, wolves put their ears back and bare their teeth when they feel in danger.

Dogs and relatives

35 species, including:

- Grey wolf, lives in North America, Europe and across Asia
- Red wolf, from south-eastern North America, now exceptionally rare
- Maned wolf, from South America
- Coyote, in North and Central America
- Jackals, 4 species in Africa, southeast Europe and southern Asia
- Dingo, from Australia
- Dhole or Asian wild dog, in India, China and Southeast Asia
- African wild dog, mainly in southern Africa
- Foxes, 21 species, worldwide except Australia

Wolves of the world

- The common or grey wolf varies in appearance across its range and is also called the timber wolf, steppe wolf, tundra wolf and plains wolf.

BEARS

Bears are large, powerful mammals that feed on a very wide range of foods, from small mammals and fish, to fruits, seeds, and roots. Most bears live in woods and forests. Different species are found from the Arctic right through to the tropical forests, mainly in the Northern Hemisphere.

The biggest bears are the northern types of the brown or grizzly bear, and the polar bear. These huge animals are sometimes a danger to people, especially when protecting their young or cubs. European brown bears are smaller and found in a few isolated mountains.

CREAMY CAMOUFLAGE
The creamy white fur of the polar bear blends in well with its snowy and icy habitat, and undoubtedly helps this species to stalk seals on the ice

BEAR OF MANY NAMES
The brown bear is known by different names in different regions, including the grizzly, Eurasian brown bear, Kodiak bear, and Alaskan bear.

Asian or Himalayan black bear

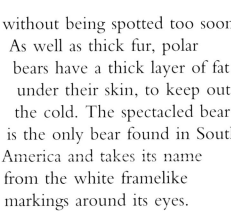

SNOW DEN
The mother polar bear rears her cubs in a cave she digs in the snow. She may not leave it for weeks, surviving on her supplies of body fat.

without being spotted too soon. As well as thick fur, polar bears have a thick layer of fat under their skin, to keep out the cold. The spectacled bear is the only bear found in South America and takes its name from the white framelike markings around its eyes.

Bears

7 species:

- Polar bear, on the Arctic tundra, coasts, and ice floes
- Brown bear, across North America, Europe and Asia, in woods and forest
- American black bear, from North American woodland
- Asian or Himalayan black bear, in Southeast Asian scrub and forest
- Sun bear, from the forests of Southeast Asia (especially Malaya)
- Sloth bear, in India and Sri Lanka, lives in forests
- Spectacled bear, in South America, especially the damp forests in the Andes

Bear records

- Smallest is the sun bear, about 4 feet (1.2 m) long.
- Largest is the polar bear, at 10 feet (3 m) long and weighing more than 1,300 pounds (590 kg).

SMALLER CARNIVORES

The mongooses and their relatives, the civets and genets, are slender-bodied carnivores found in Europe, Africa and south Asia. In build they seem to be a combination if weasel and cat. The common genet has a spotted body and striped tail. It comes out at night and climbs trees as it hunts for birds, reptiles and other prey. Genets are found as far north as France, but are rarely seen.

TOO FAST

Mongooses live mainly in dry country and include snakes in their diet. They even eat poisonous snakes such as cobras. The mongoose is not especially immune to the poison. It uses its lightning reflexes and agility to avoid the snake's fangs.

One of the most famous kinds of mongoose is the

MEERKATS
Also called suricates, these mongooses live in very dry areas, even the Kalahari and Namib Deserts.

grey meerkat of South West Africa. Meerkats live in colonies and post individuals as lookouts. These guards suddenly sit bolt upright when they sense danger, and alert the other members of the group.

VEGETARIAN CARNIVORES?

The red panda is related to the giant panda, but is much smaller, with deep red fur and a fox-like shape. In common with its more famous relative, the giant panda, it lives in China, and

RACCOON
Raccoons are well-known in North America, where they raid dustbins for scraps, mostly at night. They use their front paws rather like hands to find and manipulate food.

Some groups of smaller mammal carnivores:

Mongooses, civets and relatives
66 species
Including:
True civets and genets
9 species
Mongooses
27 species

Raccoons, pandas and relatives
17 species
Including:
Raccoons
6 species
Coatis
3 species
Kinkajou
1 species
Pandas
2 species

also in some other Himalayan countries. It, too, prefers bamboo forests. Although these pandas are vegetarian in diet, they are included in the carnivore mammal group because of their body similarities with other carnivores.

MUSTELIDS

The mustelids are a large group of smaller mammalian hunters with long bodies, fast reactions, and voracious appetites for meat. The weasel is a specialist hunter of small rodents such as voles and mice, though it occasionally eats birds, frogs, and even young rabbits. Its small size, slim body and narrow head enable the weasel to follow prey as small as mice into their burrows. Stoats are about twice the size of weasels and have a black tip to their tail.

Sable

MORE MUSTELIDS

Pine martens are exceptionally good at climbing and can even catch squirrels. The related sable is found in Siberian forests. It resembles the pine marten but has longer legs and larger ears. The sable produces a fine quality fur and has been both hunted and bred on farms for its pelt.

BADGER

Each badger's face stripes are slightly different, allowing these animals to recognize each other even in darkness. Badgers dig large burrows called setts (or sets), with different chambers for sleeping, resting, and eating. They keep the sett very clean, changing the bedding of grass, leaves, and moss every few days.

THE GLUTTON

Wolverines are the largest mustelids. They have broad footpads and move quickly even over loose snow. Wolverines have a legendary appetite, earning them the nickname "glutton," and kill prey as large as a reindeer. They also eat carrion and cover up to 25 miles (40 km) each day in search of food.

Badgers are also large mustelids. They are mainly nocturnal. They live in family groups but usually forage individually, following well-used tracks. Their food includes earthworms, beetles, small mammals, carrion, roots, and fruits.

WEASEL
This tiny yet fierce carnivore is so slim, it is supposed to be able to slip through a ring that would fit snugly on a human finger.

White underside

More groups of smaller mammal carnivores:

Weasels, stoats, polecats, ferrets, martens, mink, and similar predators (mustelids)
33 species

Skunks
13 species

Otters
12 species

Badgers
8 species

Another group of related carnivores:

Hyenas
4 species
- spotted hyena lives in Africa south of the Sahara desert
- striped hyena lives in Africa, Middle East, and southern Asia to India
- brown hyena lives in Central and Southern Africa

BATS

The bats, or chiropterans, form the second-largest mammal group in terms of numbers of species, after rodents. They are the only mammals which can truly fly. There are two main types of bats. These are the large, often day-flying fruit bats and flying foxes, and the mostly small, insect-eating bats which are nearly all nocturnal (active at night).

BAT FOOD

A few bats have specialized foods. Some catch small birds, others swoop over water to grab fish. Vampire bats feed on blood, but, contrary to legend, they are rarely dangerous to people. Vampire bats live in Central and South

HORSESHOE BAT
A bat's arms are adapted for flight. The fingers have very long bones which hold out the wings, made of very thin, elastic skin. The bat's body is very light, and its claws are adapted for hanging at the roost.

ECHOLOCATION
Most bats find their way in the dark by echolocation. They send out very high-pitched (ultrasonic) clicks and squeaks. These reflect or bounce off objects. The bat hears the returning echoes and works out the distance, size and shape of the objects.

America, are quite small, and only one kind attacks mammals such as sleeping cattle, pigs or horses. The bat makes a small wound with its sharp teeth, then licks up the blood which oozes out. Most bats rest and sleep in colonies, hanging upside down.

Roosting bat

Fox-eared bat   Horseshoe bat   Vampire bat

BAT FACES
Each main type of bat has slightly different facial features, linked to the way it feeds or finds its way by echolocation.

Bats
960 species
• only mammals with true powered flight
• front limbs are modified as wings
• use echolocation in flight
• most are nocturnal

Some groups of bats:
Flying foxes and fruit bats
175 species
Common or vesper bats
320 species
Spear-nosed bats
140 species
Free-tailed bats
90 species
Horseshoe bats
70 species
Leaf-nosed bats
60 species
Vampire bats
3 species

33

INSECT EATERS

The insect eaters or insectivores are mostly rather small mammals, and include shrews, moles, and hedgehogs. Most are nocturnal, and their sensitive noses help them find their way about and track down prey.

SHARP TEETH

The teeth of shrews and similar insectivores are quite different from those of mice. Whereas rodents have long, chisel-like, cutting teeth, a shrew has very sharp teeth, more like those of a miniature cat. Shrews are so small, yet so active, that they must eat food every few hours, or they starve to death.

Moles are well adapted to their subterranean life, with a cylindrical body, short limbs, and soft, silky fur that allows them to slither easily through the soil. Moles use their spadelike front limbs to dig their underground tunnels. Every so often,

COMMON HEDGEHOG

The spines of a hedgehog are modified hairs, and a fully grown hedgehog has about 16,000. They normally lie flat along the body, but they can be raised, using powerful muscles, when the hedgehog is alarmed. With its head and legs tucked into its belly, the hedgehog rolls into a spiny ball. This deters most predators but is, sadly, no defense against road traffic!

they heave the loose soil to the surface through vertical tunnels to make the familiar molehills. A mole's tunnel system may stretch for up to 500 feet (160 m). A much larger molehill, the fortress, covers the mole's resting and breeding chamber.

WATER SHREW
An excellent swimmer, the water shrew hunts tadpoles, small fish, and young frogs, as well as worms.

MOLE
The mole's tunnel system is its feeding place. The mole patrols the tunnels several times daily, eating worms, beetles, and other insects that have emerged through the walls. It stores excess food in a special larder chamber.

Insect eaters (insectivores)
345 species
• eat mainly insects, but also other small animals such as worms, spiders, and slugs
• mostly small and active
• long, narrow snout
• small limbs and ears
• many are nocturnal, with large eyes and long whiskers

Groups include:
Shrews
246 species
Tenrecs and otter shrews
33 species
Moles and relatives
29 species
Golden moles
18 species
Hedgehogs and moonrats
17 species
Solenodons
2 species

ARMADILLOS AND SLOTHS

These animals are often known as the toothless mammals: they either lack teeth altogether, or their teeth are small and simple, and not firmly rooted. Anteaters have a long snout, long sticky tongue and sharp claws. They rip open the nests of ants or termites, then lick up the insects in their hundreds. Armadillos resemble anteaters which have been armour-plated. Their skin is covered by protective bony plates, and they can tuck in their limbs and roll up into a hard ball if attacked.

A SLOW LIFE

Sloths take their name from their very slow movements. These inhabitants of South American rainforests spend most of their lives suspended upside-down from tree branches, feeding on

ARMADILLO
This armoured mammal eats ants, termites and other small invertebrates, and also other food such as fruit. It lives in South and Central America, and the southern US. The smaller pink fairy armadillo, only 12 centimetres long, dwells in South America.

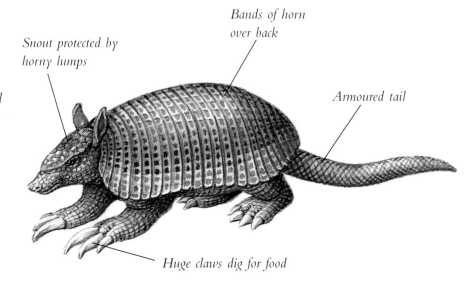

Snout protected by horny lumps

Bands of horn over back

Armoured tail

Huge claws dig for food

Three-toed sloth

fruit and leaves. They are often disguised among the leaves by the tiny green plants (algae) growing in their dense fur. Even the sloth's digestion is slow. It can take a month for a meal to pass through the sloth's body.

Hooked claws cling to branches

PANGOLIN
This nocturnal climber searches for ants and termites among the branches. Pangolins live in Africa, southern and Southeast Asia.

Overlapping horny scales

Toothless mammals
29 species
• slow-moving
• most have long claws
• very simple teeth, or no teeth

Groups include:
Armadillos
20 species
Sloths
5 species
Anteaters
4 species
Pangolins
7 species
Aardvark
1 species

Long tongue
The tongue of the giant anteater is 60 centimetres long, and can collect hundreds of termites or ants with a single lick. The anteater may eat tens of thousands of ants in a single day.

RABBITS AND HARES

 Rabbits and hares have long ears and short tails. They also have long back legs that they use for hopping and also for running and leaping at great speed. Although they resemble rodents, rabbits and hares have their own mammal group, lagomorphs, meaning "leaping shapes."

LIFE IN THE OPEN
Many rabbits and hares live in open, grassy country where they need their speed to take them clear of their enemies. Hares are the fastest, reaching speeds of 50 miles per hour (80 km/h). They have strong teeth and can gnaw and chew hard seeds, roots, and bark. The position of the eyes, on the sides of the head, gives rabbits and hares good all-round vision, even when keeping their heads perfectly still. They can even see

EUROPEAN RABBIT
This rabbit has become a serious pest in many parts of the world. In one year, a single female can produce more than 20 young, and these begin to breed themselves when only four months old. However, many animals hunt rabbits, from eagles to foxes and stoats.

behind themselves. Their large ears can quickly pick out any sound and they are ever alert to danger. Rabbits tend to live in systems of tunnels dug into the soil, but most hares have their babies on the surface of the ground.

Pikas are small, rabbitlike mammals with rounded ears and almost no tail. They live in mountainous country in Asia and northwest North America.

COTTONTAIL
This rabbit rarely digs its own burrow. It takes over another animal's, or rests in a sheltered place on the surface, called a form.

Rabbits and hares (lagomorphs)
44 species
- large ears
- long hind legs
- eyes face sideways
- very short tail
- slit-like nostrils

Pikas
14 species
- rounded ears
- almost tail-less
- resemble large voles

Rabbit or hare?
- The American jackrabbit is actually a species of hare.
- Like other hares it has large ears. It uses these to hear, and also to regulate its temperature. In hot weather the ears give off body warmth, keeping the hare cool.
- In North America, some kinds of rabbits are known as cottontails.

SEA MAMMALS

Whales and dolphins are the mammals most perfectly adapted to life at sea. They never come ashore (unless beached by accident) and cannot survive on land. The baleen whales, which are mostly large, feed by filtering tiny organisms from the sea. The toothed whales include the sperm whale, which eats mainly squid, and the many kinds of dolphins and porpoises.

SEAL OR SEA-LION?

Seals and sea-lions are also at home in the open sea, but they come ashore to bask and breed, either on rocky coasts or on open ice. Seals eat a range of prey, from fish and birds to crabs and squid.

The true seals have back flippers which cannot be bent under the body to walk on land. They slide or slither on the ground, but swim with

SEA-LION
Most species of sea-lions live in groups. They come ashore at traditional breeding places called rookeries, where the males battle with each other to win the attention of females.

Nostrils to breathe air

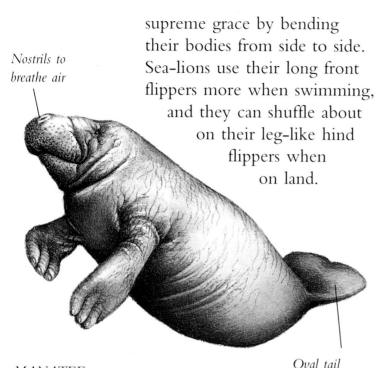

supreme grace by bending their bodies from side to side. Sea-lions use their long front flippers more when swimming, and they can shuffle about on their leg-like hind flippers when on land.

Oval tail fluke

MANATEE

The manatees and dugongs (both known as sea-cows) are gentle herbivores. They swim slowly in tropical seas and estuaries, grazing on water plants and algae.

TUSKED SWIMMER

The walrus is one of the giants of the group. It has long tusks, and a very fat body to keep out the cold of the Arctic Ocean. A large male walrus may be almost four metres long. It uses its tusks to lever shellfish from the seabed.

main groups of marine (sea-dwelling) mammals:

- **Whales and dolphins (cetaceans)**
  76 species
  Includes:
- **Toothed whales, dolphins and porpoises**
  66 species
- **Baleen or great whales**
  10 species

- **Seals and sea-lions (pinnipeds)**
  34 species
  Includes:
- **True seals**
  19 species
- **Fur seals and sea-lions**
  14 species
- **Walrus**
  1 species

- **Manatees and dugong (sea-cows or sirenians)**
  4 species

PIGS, RHINOS, AND HIPPOS

 The hoofed mammals, or ungulates, range in size from tiny deer to huge rhinos and hippos. Their key features are toes that end in clublike hooves rather than sharp claws. They are divided into two main groups, the even-toed or cloven-hoofed ungulates (artiodactyls) and the odd-toed ungulates (perissodactyls).

GRUBBING ABOUT

Pigs are well-known farmyard animals, but the wild ancestors of the domestic pig are the wild boars—which look rather different! Wild boars have much thicker coats and larger heads. They are still common in forests in many parts of Europe and Asia.

Most wild pigs have tusks, formed from up-curved canine teeth. They grub about in the soil for roots, bulbs and small animals. Peccaries resemble wild pigs and are found in forests of South and Central America.

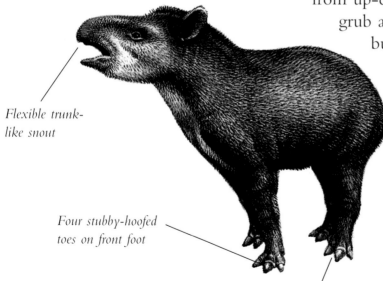

Flexible trunk-like snout

Four stubby-hoofed toes on front foot

Three hoofed toes on back foot

TAPIR
Three of the four tapir species live in South America. The fourth comes from Southeast Asia. Tapirs are active at night, eating leaves, fruits, and other plant food in their forest homes.

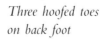

RHINOS
The horn of a rhino is not bone or even horn. It is a dense matted mass of compressed body hairs. Most species of rhinos, especially the Asian ones, are extremely rare.

HIPPOS, BIG AND SMALL

There are two different kinds of hippos, both living wild in Africa. The larger species, familiar in wildlife parks and zoos, spends much of its life submerged in rivers or lakes. It emerges at night to graze on soft waterside plants and grasses. The other, the much smaller pygmy hippo, is a rare animal of swampy forests.

WILD BOAR
Stocky and powerful, the wild boar may charge if provoked. Its slashing tusks can cause deep wounds.

Hoofed mammals (ungulates) are divided into:

Odd-toed (perissodactyls)
These consist of:
Rhinos
5 species
Tapirs
4 species
Asses, horses, and zebras
7 species

Even-toed (artiodactyls)
These consist of:
Camels and llamas
6 species
Wild pigs
9 species
Peccaries
3 species
Hippos
2 species
Giraffes
2 species
Deer
41 species
Wild cattle, antelopes, sheep, and goats
124 species

43

DEER AND ANTELOPES

Deer and antelopes are long-legged, browsing or grazing, hoofed mammals. They have the typical flattened teeth of a herbivore, for grinding up plants, and special stomachs to help them digest their food. They tend to live in herds for safety and they can run fast when chased. The main feature of deer is their antlers, which can be many-branched and are shed and regrown each year. In most species it is only the male deer which carries antlers, but in reindeer both sexes have them.

Broad-bladed antlers

NOT ANTLERS
Antelopes have horns, not antlers, and these grow throughout their lives. In some antelopes the horns are very short, but in others, such as the sable antelope, they are long and curved.

MALE FALLOW DEER
These deer feed mainly at dawn and dusk. During the middle of the day and night, they rest in undergrowth or among trees, where their spotted coats provide camouflage. The background coat colour varies from very dark brown, through chestnut and pale fawn, to nearly white.

Antelopes are well known for their speed and agility, and their keen eyesight usually gives them early warning of an attack by their predators. Some antelopes confuse their pursuers by rapid changes of direction, or by suddenly jumping vertically upwards.

Reindeer with newly grown antlers

Ringed horns

IBEX
A goat-like animal, the ibex lives at heights of up to 3,000 metres in the Alps of Europe.

Cloven (two-toed) hoof

Some groups of even-toed ungulates:

Deer
41 species
• Includes red deer, fallow deer, sika, roe, reindeer or caribou, elk or moose, muntjac

Gazelles and dwarf antelopes
30 species
• Includes Grant's gazelle, Thomson's gazelle, dikdik

Grazing antelopes
24 species
• Includes pronghorn, waterbuck, wildebeest or gnu, impala, sable antelope, oryx

Spiral-horned antelopes
9 species
• Includes kudus and elands

Pronghorn
1 species

WILD CATTLE

The mighty bison once roamed the forests over the whole of Europe, but retreated to remote wooded areas as the land increasingly came under cultivation. By the beginning of this century they were almost extinct, but have now been reintroduced in some places.

The closely related North American bison or buffalo was similarly almost exterminated in its prairie home, before being rescued.

WILD CATTLE

Until the seventeenth century, there were also wild cattle in Europe and Asia. They were a species known as the auroch—the ancestor of all domesticated cattle.

Cattle and goats probably began their domestication about 9,000 years ago, for their milk, meat, fur, and hides. This means they are among the earliest of all domesticated animals.

Small horns

TAKIN
Also known as the golden-fleeced cow, this small species of wild cattle stands only 3 feet (1 m) tall at the shoulder. It lives in the high, dense, remote bamboo forests of Southeast Asia and China.

Thick, shaggy, golden fur

Powerful legs

46

LONGEST FUR

Musk oxen have extremely thick, furry coats to protect themselves from the fiercest Arctic storms. Their hair is longer than that of any other wild animal, reaching 36 inches (90 cm) on the neck and flanks.

YAK
The bulky yak lives in the Tibetan highlands, at heights up to 20,000 feet (6,000 m). Herds of yak have been domesticated by local people.

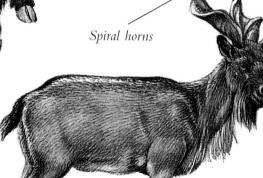

Spiral horns

Himalayan markhor

More groups of even-toed ungulates:

Cattle and relatives
23 species
• Includes domestic cattle, yak, water buffalo, African buffalo, American bison (buffalo), European bison

Sheep, goats and relatives
26 species
• Includes saiga, musk ox, chamois, ibex, Spanish ibex, markhor, mountain goat, wild goat, Barbary sheep, mouflon, bighorn sheep

Biggest horns
The water buffalo, native to India and Southeast Asia, has the largest horns of any living animal. The record spread, from one horn-tip to the other, is more than 13 feet (4 m).

GIRAFFES AND HORSES

Two further groups of hoofed mammals or ungulates are the horses, asses and zebras (odd-toed), and the giraffe and closely-related but very rare okapi (even-toed).

Domesticated horses are familiar on farms, racecourses, cross-country events and showgrounds. All the breeds, from tiny Shetlands to giant Shires, belong to one species, *Equus caballus*. They are probably descended from wild horses similar to today's only semi-wild species, Przewalski's horse of Mongolia. Zebras are very similar to horses in build and habits, being wary, long-legged, fast-running animals of open grassland.

THE TALLEST MAMMALS

The giraffe and the okapi are both very unusual animals. Giraffes are easy to spot in their open savanna habitat

WHY STRIPES?
Each of the three kinds of zebra – plains, mountain and Grevy's – has a different stripe pattern. The stripes are like fingerprints, unique in each animal. They may help individuals in the herd to recognize each other, and with camouflage in the long African grass.

48

in Africa, as they tower above other animals on their long legs, using their long necks and long tongues to reach the topmost twigs and leaves.

The related okapi, also with a longish neck, looks like a combination of giraffe and zebra. It is a shy inhabitant of West African rainforest and is seldom seen in the wild.

GIRAFFE VARIETIES
There are several different varieties of the single giraffe species, each with a different brown and white coat pattern.

More groups of hoofed mammals (ungulates):

Horses, asses and zebras
7 species
Including:

Horses
2 species
• Domestic
• Przewalski's

Wild asses
2 species
• African
• Asian

Zebras
3 species
• Plains
• Mountain
• Grevy's

Giraffes
2 species
• Giraffe
• Okapi

Record height
• Giraffes may grow to almost 6 metres, making them by far the tallest mammals.

CAMELS AND LLAMAS

The camel group of even-toed hoofed mammals includes two kinds of camels. It also includes the domesticated llamas and alpacas, and the wild guanacos and vicunas, which all live in South America.

Wild two-humped or bactrian camels can still be found in some parts of the remote steppe grasslands of Mongolia. They live in dry, sandy habitats and can go for weeks between drinks.

The one-humped or dromedary camels of southwest Asia and North Africa are mostly domesticated, used for centuries for transportation, milk, and meat.

A camel's hump stores not water, but body fat, to help the animal through times of food shortage.

Domesticated llama

PRECIOUS WATER
Camels do not have a magical ability to store water. But they can survive long periods between drinks. When they do find water, they can take in 13 gallons (50 l) at once, since the camel's stomach can expand enormously. They also lose very little moisture as sweat, and produce concentrated urine, which also saves water.

WOOL AND TRANSPORTATION

In South America, both the llama and alpaca have been domesticated as pack animals and also for their wool. The vicuna is a smaller version of the llama and lives at heights of more than 13,000 feet (4,000 m) on the Andes Mountains. It was rare but is now a protected species.

DESERT LIFE
The camel has many adaptations to desert survival. Most one-humped or dromedary camels are domesticated or semiwild.

Large eyelashes keep out windblown sand

Food store in hump

Wide feet do not sink in soft sand

Nostrils can be almost closed in sandstorms

Thick fur protects against sun's heat

Camels and llamas

6 species

- Dromedary, Arabian or one-humped camel, is mainly domesticated, lives across North Africa and the Middle East; also populations introduced as pack animals in other dry places, such as Australia; now run semiwild
- Bactrian or two-humped camel, lives semiwild or domesticated on Mongolian grasslands
- Llama lives in the Andes region of South America, in grassland and shrubland; used for transportation, meat, wool, milk, and skins
- Alpaca is similar to llama but smaller in size; lives slightly higher in the Andes
- Guanaco is widespread at lower altitudes through South America
- Vicuna lives on high Andes, in Peru, Bolivia, Chile, and Argentina

MONKEYS AND LEMURS

The lemurs, monkeys and apes make up the mammal group called primates. They have a large brain, well-developed hands with a flexible thumb for grasping objects, and large eyes which both face forwards, giving good vision to judge distances accurately.

OLD WORLD MONKEYS

Over 80 different kinds of monkey live in Africa and Asia. One of the commonest in Africa is the vervet monkey, equally at home on the ground or in trees.

Baboons are large, ground-dwelling monkeys with dog-like faces and sharp teeth. Although most monkeys live in tropical areas, some, such as the hanuman langur, a common species in India, can also be found high in the mountains.

SPIDER MONKEY
The New World or American monkeys have a prehensile tail, which is used as a fifth limb for grasping branches.

LANGUR
Langurs have adapted well to human habitation and raid rubbish tips and picnic sites for food.

LEMURS

Lemurs are found only in Madagascar. These monkey-like animals are mostly nocturnal and feed on fruits, seeds, flowers and leaves, gathered as they move through the trees. They have large eyes and ears, pointed noses and soft, attractive fur. The ring-tailed lemur is a popular animal in wildlife parks and zoos.

TITI MONKEY
Most monkeys eat a varied diet of flowers, fruits, seeds, insects and other small animals, and bird and reptile eggs.

Lemurs, bushbabies, monkeys and apes (Primates)

The group includes:

Old World monkeys (Africa and Asia)
82 species

New World or American monkeys
30 species

Marmosets and tamarins
21 species

Lemurs
22 species

Bushbabies and lorises
10 species

Tarsiers
3 species

Aye-aye
1 species

Apes are shown in the next pages.

53

APES

The lesser apes include nine kinds of gibbons from Southeast Asia. They are incredibly agile climbers, using their long, muscular arms to swing themselves through the trees. They communicate with other members of their group by loud, musical cries which echo through their forest home.

There are four species of great apes. Best known are the chimpanzee and gorilla, from restricted areas in Africa. Chimps are clever animals and have been observed to use sticks and other tools to help themselves find food. They take a wide range of items, from nuts and fruit, to other animals such as lizards and small monkeys.

The pygmy chimp, or bonobo, is much rarer and less known than the chimp.

GORILLAS
The large senior male of a gorilla group, known as the silverback, protects the others and will charge at an attacker. But most of the time, gorillas live quiet, peaceful lives.

IN THE TREES
*Full-grown chimps are
as heavy as people and
spend much time on
the ground.
Youngsters play
in the branches
as they learn to
find food.*

Gorillas are huge,
muscular apes and
are almost entirely vegetarian. They live in
small groups in dense forest, feeding mainly
on the leaves and stems of forest trees and
vines. Orangutans live in the forests of
Borneo and Sumatra. They are very fond
of fruit.

More groups of primates:

Gibbons (lesser apes)
9 species
Includes:
- agile gibbon
- kloss gibbon
- lar gibbon
- siamang

Great apes
4 species
Includes:
- chimpanzee
- pygmy chimpanzee (bonobo)
- gorilla
- orangutan

Biggest primate
- The gorilla can grow to 6 feet (1.8 m) tall and weigh 400 pounds (180 kg).
- Humans are also included in the primate group. Evidence from fossils, evolution, and genetics shows that our closest living relatives are chimps.

SAVING WILDLIFE

As the pressures on the natural world increase, especially due to our growing human populations, the wildlife of the planet becomes ever more threatened. Such pressures include pollution of the environment from industry, traffic and agricultural chemicals, and the destruction of forests, grassland, wetlands and other habitats to create farmland, housing and roads.

There are still many wild places left on earth where plants and animals flourish almost unhindered, such as the open Siberian tundra and boreal forests. But the richest places for wildlife are also some of the most threatened – particularly the moist lowland tropical forests, which contain far more species than anywhere else, but which disappear at an alarming rate. In highly populated temperate

regions, such as western Europe, there are few natural habitats left, and any remnants are therefore very precious.

FAMILIAR BUT ALMOST GONE

Many animals familiar to us from zoos and wildlife parks are under real threat in their natural homes. Examples are black rhinos, the great apes (orang-utans, chimpanzees and gorillas), tigers, and that famous symbol of conservation, the giant panda. Without adequate protection of their habitats, these species (and many others) are almost certainly doomed to extinction.

HUNTING

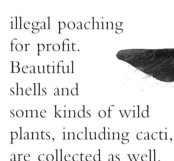

People have hunted animals and collected wild plants for thousands of years. In the early days of human evolution, it was necessary to survive. Nowadays, however, hunting continues mostly as a sport, or in more sinister fashion as illegal poaching for profit. Beautiful shells and some kinds of wild plants, including cacti, are collected as well.

HUNTING AT SEA

The large whales were hunted almost to the point of no return for their meat, oil, and fat. In the 1980s, most countries halted this activity and whale populations now show signs of recovery. Dolphins, smaller cousins of the whales, suffer from being snared in fishing nets and many die accidentally by drowning.

SUCCESS STORY?

Begun in the 1960s, Operation Tiger planned to save these big cats. But in the 1980s, it was discovered that the numbers of tigers had been deliberately recorded as too high, giving a false impression of success.

NOT SO COMMON
Common dolphins have become rare in some areas, where they suffer pollution or get trapped in nets.

THE IVORY TRADE

Hunting has had a major impact on large mammals, especially on the open plains and savannas of Africa where rhinoceroses, elephants, and others are easily spotted, and shot. The high price of ivory has fueled the illegal killing of elephants, which have become rare in many areas.

CLUBBED TO DEATH
A film of baby seals being clubbed to death for their fur offended many people around the world. Most seals are now safe, but many other animals are still treated in this way.

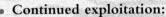

Continued exploitation:

- Live monkeys and apes, and tropical birds such as parrots, are trapped and exported, usually illegally. Many of these die in transit.
- Reptiles, such as crocodiles and alligators are trapped, and their skins exported, again illegally, for making fashion items such as handbags.
- Big cats such as tigers and leopards are still also killed for fashion, their skins finding their way eventually into hats and coats.
- Smaller and lesser-known cats are also under threat. Their illegally obtained furs are less easy to identify and trace.
- Rhinoceroses are killed for their horns. Some people believe that powdered rhino horn has medicinal powers.

SAVING SPECIES

The most effective and natural way to save threatened species is to ensure that they have sufficient and suitable places to live – their natural habitats. It is also vital to keep human pressures, such as hunting, to a minimum.

However, this is not always possible, and emergency measures may be taken to save species on the brink of extinction.

Some species have been taken into captivity and bred there to build up their populations, before being returned to the wild. Success has been achieved with the European bison, the American buffalo (bison), and also with the Arabian oryx. Przewalski's horse is another candidate. Herds of this domestic horse ancestor have been established with the hope of re-introduction to their native habitat, the Asian steppes.

SUMATRAN RHINO
Critically endangered, this species probably breeds too slowly to be saved in zoo programmes.

MEDITERRANEAN MONK SEAL
This seal is very nervous of human presence, and mothers may lose their unborn babies if disturbed. However the seal's range is becoming more crowded with holiday centres, boats and scuba-divers.

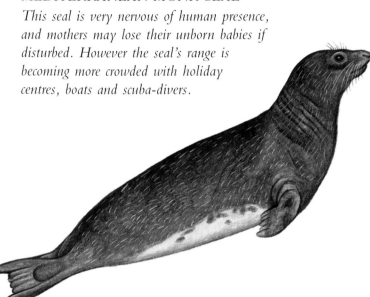

Several zoos now specialize in breeding rare species, with the hope of re-establishing them in the wild. However, zoo animals may become too dependent upon people.

GLOVED HAND
The California condor, one of the world's largest flying birds, became extinct in the wild in the late 1980s. A breeding programme has kept it going in captivity. The chicks are fed by hand, using a special glove shaped like an adult condor's head. Hopefully, the young birds will not become familiar with their keepers.

- **Just a few very rare animals:**
- **Black-footed ferret**
  USA
  - Threats are habitat loss, disease, hunting (next page)
- **Blue whale**
  All oceans
  - Main threat was hunting
- **Aye-aye**
  Madagascar
  - Main threats are deforestation, hunting
- **Golden lion tamarin**
  Brazil
  - Main threat is deforestation
- **Orang-utan**
  Borneo, Sumatra
  - Main threats are habitat loss, capture
- **Philippine eagle**
  Philippines
  - Main threats are habitat loss, hunting

INDEX

lemming 14, 15
lemur 52-53
leopard, 20, 21, 59
lion 20, 21, 23
lizard 54
llama 43, 50-51
lynx 20

M
mammal 8-61
  placental 9, 14, 15
manatee 9, 41
margay 22
markhor 47
marmot 16
marsupial 9, 10-13
meerkat 28, 29
mole 12, 13, 34, 35
mongoose 28, 29
monkey 21, 52-53,
  54, 59
monotreme 11
mouse 8, 12, 13, 14,
  15, 30, 34
musk ox 47
mustelid 30-31

O
okapi 48, 49
opossum 13
orangutan 55, 57, 61
otter 31

P
panda 29, 57

pangolin 37
panther 20
parasite 58
peccary 42, 43
pest 10
pig 33, 42-43
pika 39
pine marten 30
plant 40, 42, 43, 58
pollution 56, 59
porcupine 17
porpoise 40, 41
possum 11, 12, 13
prairie 46
prairie dog 16
puma 20, 21, 23

R
rabbit 9, 22, 30,
  38-39
racoon 29,
rain forest 36, 49
rat 12, 13, 14, 15, 22
reptile 28, 53, 59
  crocodile 59
rhinoceros 42-43, 43
  57, 59, 60
rodent 14-17, 21, 30,
  32, 34, 38

S
sable 30
sand cat 23
savanna 48
seal 40, 41, 59, 61

sea lion 40, 41
sheep 43, 47
shellfish 41
shrew 34, 35
skunk 31
sloth 21, 36-37
slug 35
snake 28; cobra 28
soil 35, 39
spider 35
steppe 25, 50
stoat 38
squid 40
squirrel 11, 14, 16,
  17, 22, 30

T
takin 46
tapir 42, 43
termite 36, 37
tiger 20, 21, 57, 58
tree 12, 16, 19, 28,
  36, 44, 53, 55;
  conifer 17
tundra 24, 25, 27, 56
turtle 21

V
vegetarian 55
vicuna 50, 51
vole 14, 15, 30

W
wallaby 10, 13
walrus 41

weasel 28, 30, 31
wetlands 56
whale 40, 58;
  baleen 40, 41; blue
  61; sperm 40
wolf 24-25
wolverine 31
wombat 9, 12, 13
worm 35
  earthworm 31

Y
yak 47

Z
zebra 43, 48, 49

ACKNOWLEDGEMENTS

The publishers wish to thank the following artists who have
contributed to this book.

David Ashby, Mike Atkinson, Wayne Ford, Roger Kent,
Stuart Lafford (Linden Artists),
Alan Male (Linden Artists), Terry Riley.

All photographs from the Miles Kelly Archive.